INTRODUCTION

Through this book, I want to share some basic principles of personal finance. The aim is to convey the basics of financial education.

This book is aimed at people who are looking for a change in their lives.

It is essential to realize that YOU are responsible for your current financial situation. Once you accept this responsibility, you will understand that YOU are also the only person who can change your financial situation.

Think of this book as a contract with yourself. You agree to follow 3 basic principles of personal finance.

I am providing you with parts of the book for you to fill in. They are in a way small exercises that will require some involvement on your part. They will help you get a clear idea of your current financial situation.

<u>Step 1</u> : Earning money

It's the preliminary stage, the base.

To do this, you absolutely must find a job quickly if you don't have one.

Whether you are unemployed or a student, find a job as soon as possible. Even if it's a job below your school level, be able to make this sacrifice : full-time work, part-time work, etc.

This is not necessarily a job in which you will make a career. It is mainly about generating money, having a regular flow of money.

This step is mainly for people who are unemployed. However, even if you are already employed, you can find a second job if you need one.

To be able to improve your personal finances, you must first earn money.

What actions do you take to find a job?

(Resume, job fairs, applications, interviews,...)

Step 2 : Managing your money

We need to track his expenses. It's a shame to see your hard-earned money slip through your fingers.

So you need to know where your money is going, to the penny!

In order to efficiently track your spending, I advise you to consult your last 3 bank statements and list all the money you have spent.

You will thus identify 3 types of expenses :
- **Necessary expenses.** These are invoices and other compulsory expenses. Examples: rent; taxes; your child's crèche; etc.
- **Compressible expenses.** These are all the expenses that you can reduce. Either by modifying them (changing suppliers) or by reducing them. Examples: telephone, internet, cable, groceries, etc.
- **Unnecessary expenses.** These are expenses you can do without. Example: a gym membership when you never go to the gym; regular purchases of clothes (your closet can't take it anymore!), etc.

If you use a lot of cash, you can either use a credit card or write down all your cash expenses in a notebook. Check your spending every week.

Once you have identified and cleaned up your expenses, you will be able to draw up your budget.

Your Bank Statement #1

Necessary expenses : list and amounts

Your Bank Statement #1

Compressible expenses : list and amounts

_____

_____

_____

_____

_____

_____

_____

_____

_____

_____

_____

_____

_____

_____

_____

_____

_____

_____

Your Bank Statement #1

Non necessary expenses : list and amounts

_____

_____

_____

_____

_____

_____

_____

_____

_____

_____

_____

_____

_____

_____

_____

_____

_____

_____

_____

_____

_____

Your Bank Statement #2

Necessary expenses : list and amounts

_____

_____

_____

_____

_____

_____

_____

_____

_____

_____

_____

_____

_____

_____

_____

_____

_____

_____

_____

_____

Your Bank Statement #2

Compressible expenses : list and amounts

_____

_____

_____

_____

_____

_____

_____

_____

_____

_____

_____

_____

_____

_____

_____

_____

_____

_____

Your Bank Statement #2

Non necessary expenses : list and amounts

_____

_____

_____

_____

_____

_____

_____

_____

_____

_____

_____

_____

_____

_____

_____

_____

_____

_____

Your Bank Statement #3

Necessary expenses : list and amounts

Your Bank Statement #3

Compressible expenses : list and amounts

_____

_____

_____

_____

_____

_____

_____

_____

_____

_____

_____

_____

_____

_____

_____

_____

_____

_____

Your Bank Statement #3

Non necessary expenses : list and amounts

_____

_____

_____

_____

_____

_____

_____

_____

_____

_____

_____

_____

_____

_____

_____

_____

_____

_____

_____

Step 3 : Define your budget

You must list your monthly budget for each of your expense items.

I generally recommend 4 major expense items:

- **Daily Expenses** are rent, groceries, water, electricity, phone, internet. Daily expenses should represent between 50% and 60% of your monthly net income.

- **The Emergency Fund** is an amount that you set aside for the unexpected. And believe me, there are always contingencies. This will allow you to face the hazards of life. I recommend between 10% and 20% of your monthly net income.

- **Hobbies and pleasure** are activities such as cinema, gym, restaurants, going out with friends, ... This expense item should be between 10% and 20% of your net monthly income.

- **Project savings** is a sum of money that you save in order to carry out one or more projects. It can be a trip, buying a car, buying your house or preparing your wedding. It can represent 20% to 30% of your net monthly income.

Once this budget is defined, you must respect it for at least the next 6 months. You will then see your bank accounts gradually turn green.

Expenses to be cut - why?

Expenses to keep - why?

Your daily expenses

Your emergency fund

Your hobbies and pleasures

Your project savings

Your new budget - month # 1

Your new budget - month #2

Your new budget - month #3

Your new budget - month #4

Your new budget - month #5

Your new budget - month #6

CONCLUSION

The steps mentioned in this book are really the basics in cleaning up personal finances.

It is important to apply each of these steps in order.

You probably dream of getting rich, of becoming financially free. But all this is impossible without sound financial management.

And better financial management will help you avoid stress. You'll be more confident in your daily life.

One of the most important lessons you can learn is that you have to live within your means.

Your new money management skills will help you in turn to advise your loved ones : family, friends, colleagues.

I wish you good luck in taking control of your personal finances and be prosperous.

www.ingramcontent.com/pod-product-compliance
Lightning Source LLC
Chambersburg PA
CBHW030603220526
45463CB00007B/3161